*For the Installation of James Gertmenian as Seni...
Minister of Plymouth Congregational Church,
Minneapolis, Minnesota, 27 October 1996*

I FIND MY FEET HAVE FURTI...

for SATB Chorus, unaccompanied

EMILY DICKINSON

LIBBY LARSEN

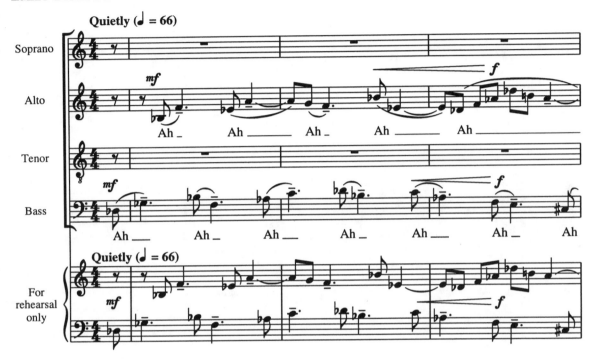

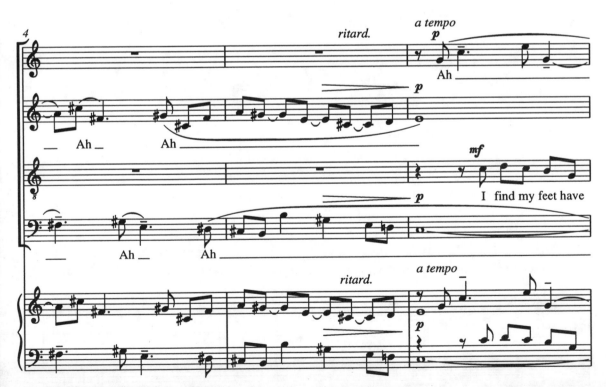

Printed in U.S.A.